Python for Beginners: The Dummies' Guide to Learn Python Programming. A Practical Reference with Exercises for Newbies and Advanced Developers

Python Programming, Volume 1

Kevin Lioy

Published by Kevin Lioy, 2024.

PYTHON FOR BEGINNERS: THE DUMMIES' GUIDE TO LEARN PYTHON PROGRAMMING. A PRACTICAL REFERENCE WITH EXERCISES FOR NEWBIES AND ADVANCED DEVELOPERS

First edition. March 4, 2024.

ISBN: 979-8224254798

Written by Kevin Lioy.

Also by Kevin Lioy

Programmazione per Principianti
Python: La Guida Per Imparare a Programmare. Include Esercizi di Programmazione.

Programmazione Web
MySQL: Database SQL per Principanti
PHP: Sviluppo Web Lato Server
NodeJS: Programmare Web-App Con Javascript

Python Programming
Python for Beginners: The Dummies' Guide to Learn Python Programming. A Practical Reference with Exercises for Newbies and Advanced Developers

WordPress Programming
WordPress for Beginners: The Complete Dummies Guide to Start Your Own Blog From Zero to Advanced Development and Customization. Includes Plugin and SEO Techniques to Kickstart Your Business.
Blogging for Beginners: The Dummies Guide to Start a Business Blog from Scratch, Become a Niche Influencer with SEO and Social Media and Profit from Affiliate Marketing

Table of Contents

Introduction

This book divulges proven steps and strategies to help beginners learn Python Programming quickly and easily. It is designed to be a practical, step-by-step tutorial of essential Python programming concepts for self-learners from beginner to intermediate level.

It uses a straightforward approach that focuses on imparting the important ideas without the heavy programming jargon. Python, after all, is a language with simple and easy-to- learn syntax.

The book features various Python programs as examples as well as a concise explanation of the different aspects of Python Programming. By the time you finish the book, you will be equipped with the necessary skills to create useful and practical codes on your own.

Chapter 1: What is Python?

Python is a broadly utilized abnormal state programming language made by Guido van Rossum in the late 1980s. The language places solid accentuation on code intelligibility and straightforwardness, making it workable for software engineers to create applications quickly.

Like all high-level programming dialects, Python code looks like the English language which PCs can't get it. Codes that we write in Python must be translated by a unique program known as the Python mediator, which we'll need to introduce before we can code, test and execute our Python programs.

There are likewise various outsider instruments, for example, Py2exe or Pyinstaller that enable us to bundle our Python code into remaining solitary executable projects for the absolute most prominent working frameworks like Windows and Mac OS. This enables us to disseminate our Python programs without requiring the clients to introduce the Python translator.

Why Learn Python?

There are an enormous number of abnormal state programming dialects accessible, for example, C, C++, and Java. The uplifting news is all abnormal state programming dialects are fundamentally the same as each other. What contrasts is principally the sentence structure, the libraries accessible and how we get to those libraries. A library is essentially an accumulation of assets and pre-composed codes that we can utilize when we compose our projects. On the off chance that you learn one language well, you can without much of a stretch get familiar with another dialect in a small amount of the time it took you to get familiar with the primary language.

Probably you are new to programming, Python is an incredible spot to begin. One of the key highlights of Python is its effortlessness, making it the perfect language for fledglings to learn. Most projects in Python require extensively less lines of code to play out a similar undertaking contrasted with different dialects, for example, C. This prompts less programming mistakes and decreases the advancement time required. Also, Python accompanies a broad accumulation of outsider assets that broaden the abilities of the language. All things considered, Python can be utilized for an enormous assortment of undertakings, for example, for work area applications, database applications, organize programming, game programming and even versatile improvement. To wrap things up, Python is a cross stage language, which implies that code composed for one working framework, for example, Windows, will function admirably on Mac OS or Linux without rolling out any improvements to the Python code.

A portion of the highlights that you may like with Python include:

• An elegant sentence structure which will make the projects so natural to peruse. Python is anything but difficult to utilize so the program will work without a great deal of bugs. In the event that you are doing specially appointed programming assignments or model advancement since it functions admirably without issues with keeping up the program.

• Has an enormous library that will work with other programming undertakings, for example, evolving documents, scanning for content, and interfacing with web servers.

• Python is extremely intelligent. This makes it simpler for you to test out little bits of code to check whether they work. You can likewise package it with an improvement situation called IDLE.

• If you might want to grow the programming language, it is anything but difficult to reach out into different modules like C or C++. Python programming can be kept running on any unit including Unix, Linux, Windows, and Mac OS X.

• The programming is free. You won't need to pay anything to download and utilize Python in your very own life. you can likewise make alterations and redistribute this item. It is under a permit, however it is an open source permit so others can utilize it.

• Even however Python is a straightforward programming language, it contains some propelled highlights like rundown cognizances and generators.

• Errors can be gotten rapidly in this programming. Since information types are powerfully composed, when you combine types that don't coordinate, it will raise a special case for you to take note.

You can bunch the codes into bundles and modules if necessary. There is a wide assortment of essential information types that you can browse including word references, records, strings, and numbers.

Python has been around for more than 29 years now and since it is probably the least demanding code to figure out how to use, there have been many various codes composed utilizing the framework. Fortunately this framework is publicly released so the code is accessible for any software engineer to utilize. You can introduce the Python program in your very own framework and use it for your very own utilization. Regardless of whether you are utilizing the codes to complete off an item or to keep in touch with your very own portion codes, the library of Python is anything but difficult to utilize. The codes that you need will be introduced into the libraries and since the program has been around for a long tie, they are going to cover basically anything you desire from mechanizing your server to making changes to an image.

Since Python is so famous, the network for Python is really enormous. There are community with heaps of systems administration and workshops accessible for this programming items and bunches of spots you can visit, both on the web and disconnected, to pose inquiries or to study the program. You might need to consider looking at a couple of these spots on the off chance that you are a tenderfoot with Python as it can assist you with learning more and even to meet some new individuals.

In the event that you are keen on beginning with coding, Python is perhaps the best alternative that you can make. It is easy to begin on and since it will take a shot at a wide range of stages, it makes certain to take a shot at your PC. Since it is anything but difficult to peruse, you will see that coding doesn't have as a test and you can make your own, or gain from others in no time.

Advantages and Disadvantages of Python

Advantages or Benefits of Python

The Python language has differentiated application in the product improvement organizations, for example, in gaming, web systems and applications, language advancement, prototyping, visual depiction applications, and so forth. This gives the language several advantages over other ones utilized in the business. A portion of its points of interest are-

Broad Support Libraries

It gives huge standard libraries that incorporate the regions like string tasks, Internet, web administration devices, working framework interfaces and conventions. The greater part of the profoundly utilized programming errands are now scripted into it, so it limits the length of the code to be written in Python.

Incorporation Feature

Python includes the Enterprise Application Integration that makes it easy to build Web benefits by conjuring COM or COBRA segments. It has great control abilities as it calls legitimately through C, C++ or Java by means of Jython. Python likewise forms XML and other markup dialects as it can keep running on all cutting edge working frameworks through same byte code.

Improved Programmer's Productivity

The language has broad help libraries and clean item arranged structures that expand from 2 to 10 times the software engineer's profitability versus utilizing the dialects like Java, VB, Perl, C, C++ and C#.

Productivity

With its solid procedure joining highlights, unit testing system and upgraded control capacities contribute towards the accellerated speed for most applications and efficiency of uses. It is an extraordinary choice for structure versatile multi-convention organize applications.

Confinements or Disadvantages of Python

Python has changed profitable highlights, and developers lean toward this language to other languages since it is anything but challenging to learn and code as well. In any case, this language has still not made its place in some processing fields that incorporates Enterprise Development Shops. Along these lines, this language may not fathom a portion of the undertaking arrangements, and constraints incorporate

Trouble in Using Other Languages

The Python users become so familiar with its highlights and its broad libraries, so they face issue in learning or taking a try at other programming idioms. Python specialists may see the pronouncing of cast "qualities" or variable "types", syntactic necessities of including wavy props or semi colons as a burdensome undertaking.

Weak in Mobile Computing

Python has made its quality on numerous work area and server stages, however it is viewed as a frail language for versatile figuring. This is the explanation not many versatile applications are worked in it like Carbonnelle.

Gets Slow in Speed

Python executes with the assistance of a mediator rather than the compiler, which makes it delayed down in light of the fact that arrangement and execution help it to work regularly. Then again, it tends to be seen that it is quick for some web applications as well.

Run-time Errors

The Python language is powerfully composed so it has many structure confinements that are accounted for by some Python engineers. It has been observed that it requires, overall, more testing time, and the blunders show up when the applications are at last run.

Underdeveloped Database Access Layers

When contrasted with innovations like JDBC and ODBC, the Python's database access layer is seen as bit immature and crude. Notwithstanding, it can't be applied in the ventures that need smooth cooperation of complex heritage information.

Installing the Python Interpreter

Before we can compose our initial Python program, we need to download the fitting translator for our PCs.

We'll be utilizing Python 3 in this book on the grounds that as expressed on the official Python site "Python 2.x is inheritance, Python 3.x is the present and fate of the language". What's more, "Python 3 takes out numerous idiosyncrasies that can superfluously entangle starting programmers".

Nonetheless, note that Python 2 is at present still rather broadly utilized. Python 2 and 3 are about 90% comparable. Subsequently on the off chance that you learn Python 3, you will probably have no issues understanding codes written in Python 2.

To introduce the mediator for Python 3, head over to https://www.python.org/downloads/. The correct version ought to be shown at the highest point of the webpage. Snap on the version for Python 3 and the product will begin downloading.

On the other hand in the event that you need to introduce an alternate version, look down the page and you will see a posting of various versions. Snap on the discharge version that you need. We will be utilizing version 3.4.2 in this book. You'll be diverted to the download page for that version.

Look down towards the finish of the page and you'll see a table posting different installers for that version. Pick the correct installer for your PC. The installer to utilize relies upon two variables:

• The working framework (Windows, Mac OS, or Linux) and

• The processor (32-bit versus 64-bit) that you are utilizing.

For example, in the event that you are utilizing a 64-bit Windows PC, you will probably be utilizing the "Windows x86-64 MSI installer". Simply click on the connection to download it. On the off chance that you download and run an inappropriate installer, no stresses. You will get a mistake message and the translator won't introduce. Just download the correct installer and you are a great idea to go.

When you have effectively introduced the mediator, you are prepared to begin coding in Python.

Utilizing the Python Shell, IDLE and Writing our FIRST program

We'll be composing our code utilizing the IDLE program that comes packaged with our Python mediator.

To do that, allows first dispatch the IDLE program. You dispatch the IDLE program like how you dispatch some other programs. For example on Windows 8, you can scan for it by composing "IDLE" in the hunt box. When it is discovered, click on IDLE (Python GUI) to dispatch it. You'll be given the Python Shell demonstrated as follows.

The Python Shell enables us to utilize Python in intuitive mode. This implies we can enter each order in turn. The Shell sits tight for an order from the user, executes it and returns the aftereffect of the execution. After this, the Shell hangs tight for the following direction.

Try by typing the following into the Shell. The lines beginning with >>> are the directions you should type while the lines after the directions demonstrate the outcomes.

>>> 2+3

5

>>> 3>2

True

>>> print ('Hello World') Hello World

When you type 2+3, you are giving a direction to the Shell, soliciting it to assess the incentive from 2+3. Consequently, the Shell restores the appropriate response 5. When you type 3>2, you are inquiring as to whether 3 is more noteworthy than 2. The Shell answers True. At long last, print is a direction requesting that the Shell show the line Hello World.

The Python Shell is an advantageous instrument for testing Python directions, particularly when we are first beginning with the language. In any event that you exit from the Python Shell and enter it once more, each one of the directions you type will be no more. Also, you cannot utilize the Python Shell to create a genuine program. To code a genuine program, you have to compose your code in a book document and spare it with a .py expansion. This record is known as a Python script.

To make a Python script, click on File > New File in the top menu of our Python Shell. This will raise the word processor that we are going to use to compose our absolute first program, the "Welcome World" program. Composing the "Welcome World" program is somewhat similar to the soul changing experience for every single new software engineer. We'll be utilizing this program to acclimate ourselves with the IDLE programming.

Input the following into the text editor .

#Prints the Words "Hello World" print ("Hi World")

The line #Prints the Words "Hi World" (in red) is not a part of the program but a feedback written to make our code more readable for other programmers and users. This line is overlooked by the Python interpreter and add comments to our program, we type a # sign in front of each line of comment:

You should see that the line #Prints the Words "Hi World" is in red while "print" is in purple and "Hi World" is in green. This is the product's method for making our code simpler to peruse. The words "print" and "Hi World" fill various needs in our program, thus they are shown utilizing various colors.

#This

is

a comment

#This

is

also a comment

In another way, we can decide to use three single quotes (or three double quotes) for a multiline comments, just like this:

'''

This

is

a comment

This

is

also a comment.

'''

You can now click File > Save As… to store your code. Be sure that you save it with the extension .py.

Are you done? Voilà! You have just successfully written your 1st program in python.

Finally, click on Run > Run Module to run the program or simply press F5. You can now see the words Hello World printed on your Python Shell.

Terms You Should Know with Python

Before you get too so much into your programming with Python, it is critical to see a portion of the words that can make the programming clearer. This section is going to set aside some effort to take a gander at the various words that are basic in Python programming, and which we do discuss a piece in this manual, to help maintain a strategic distance from some perplexity and allows you to begin with your first code.

• Class—this is a format that was utilized for making client characterized objects.

• Docstring—this is a string that will show up lexically first articulation inside a module, capacity, or class definition. The object will be accessible to documentation devices.

• Function—this is a square of code that is summoned when utilizing a calling program. It is best utilized so as to give a figuring or a self-governing help.

• IDLE—this represents Integrated Development Environment for Python. It is an essential mediator and manager condition that you can use alongside Python. It is useful for the individuals who are simply starting with this and can work for those on a spending limit. It is a reasonable case of code and won't burn through a ton of time or space.

• Immutable—this is an object inside the code that is appointed a fixed worth. This could incorporate tuples, strings, and numbers. You can't adjust the object and you should make another object with an alternate worth and store it first. This can be useful sometimes, for example, the keys in a word reference.

• Interactive—one thing that a ton of apprentices like about Python is that it is so intelligent. You can evaluate some various things in the mediator and perceive how they will respond immediately in the outcomes. It is a decent method to improve your programming aptitudes, try out another thought you have and then some.

• List—this is a data type inside Python that is inherent. It contains an impermanent succession of values that are arranged. It can incorporate permanent values of numbers and strings also.

• Mutable—these are the objects that will have the option to change their incentive inside the program, however which can keep their unique id ().

• Object—inside Python, this is any data with a state, for example, a worth or a quality, just as a characterized conduct, or a strategy.

• Python 3000— The Python 2 and Python 3 are the principle two types of Python that are accessible. Numerous individuals have stayed with Python 2 since Python 3 doesn't have any regressive abilities and they like utilizing the databases on the more established form. Python 3000 is a legendary choice of Python that allows this regressive ability so you can utilize it and the Python 2.

• String—this is one of the most fundamental types that you will discover in Python that will store the content. In Python 2, the strings will store message with the goal that the string type would then be able to be utilized to clutch double data.

• Triple cited string—this is a string that has three examples of either the single statement or the twofold statement. It could have something like " I cherish tacos' '. They are utilized for some reasons. They can assist you with having twofold and single statements in a string and they make it simpler to go over a couple of lines of code without issues.

• Tuple—this is a data type that has been incorporated with Python. This data type is a changeless arranged succession of values. The grouping is the main part that is unchanging. It can contain some impermanent values, for example, having a lexicon inside it, where the values can change.

• Type—this is a class or kind of data that is spoken to in the programming dialects. These types will contrast in their properties, they including changeless and variable alternatives, just as in their capacities and strategies. Python incorporates a couple of these including word reference types, tuple, list, coasting point, long, whole number, and string.

Presently the time has come to become more acquainted with more about Python programming and how you can make it work for you. You should gain proficiency with more about the various watchwords and the factors that accompany Python so you can compose the words that you need and make the program perform with a particular goal in mind. We should investigate a portion of these nuts and bolts of Python programming so you can begin with your new code immediately.

Keywords

When you are taking a shot at another PC coding program, you are going to see that every coding languages will have certain catchphrases. These are the words that are intended for a particular direction or reason in the language and you should attempt to abstain from utilizing them anyplace else. In the event that you do utilize these words in different pieces of your code, you may wind up with a blunder alert or the program not working appropriately. The watchwords that are saved for Python include:

· None

· And

· Pass

· Or

· not

· Nonlocal

· Lambda

· Is

· In

· For

· Finally

· False

· Except

· Import

- If

- Global

- From

- Break

- Assert

- Else

- Elif

- Del

- Def

- Continue

- Class

- While

- Try

- True

- Return

- Raise

- As

- Yield

- With

The World of Variables and Operators

Since we're finished with the early on stuff, we should get down to the genuine stuff. Factors and administrators will be talked about in subtleties. In particular, you'll realize what factors mean and how to appropriately name and pronounce them. We'll likewise find out about the regular activities that we can perform on them. Are you game? We should go.Variables refer to the names given to data that we require to store and manipulate in our programs. For example, on the off chance that your program needs to store the age of a client. To achieve that, we should name this data userAge and characterize the variable userAge utilizing the accompanying articulation.

userAge = 0

After defining the variable userAge, your program will allocate a certain portion of your computer's storage space to store this data. Then you can access and modify this data by referring to it by its name, userAge. When you declare a new variable anytime, you need to give it an initial value.

In this example, we assigned to it the value 0. We can also decide to change this value in our program later. Also, we can define multiple variables at one go. To do that simply, write

userAge, userName = 30, 'Paul'

This is equivalent to

userAge = 30 userName = 'Paul'

A variable name in Python can just contain letters (a - z, A - B), numbers or underscores (_). In any condition or case, the main character can't be a number. Thus, you can name your factors userName, user_name or userName2 yet not 2userName.

What's more, there are some reserved words that you can't use as a variable name since they as of now have pre-doled out implications in Python. These saved words incorporate words like print, input, if, while and so forth.

At long last, variable names are case sensitive. username isn't equivalent to userName.

There are two shows when naming a variable in Python. We can either utilize the camel case notation or use underscores. Camel case is the act of composing compound words with mixed casing (for example thisIsAVariableName). This is the show that we'll be utilizing with in the remainder of the book. On the other hand, another basic practice is to utilize underscores (_) to isolate the words. In the event that you like, you can name your variables like this: this_is_a_variable_name.

Identifier Names

When you are making another program in Python, you are getting down to business on making many substances, a mix of capacities, classes, and factors. All of these will be given a name that is otherwise called an identifier. There are a couple of guidelines that you have to pursue when shaping an identifier in Python including:

It ought to contain letters, either capitalized or lowercase or a blend

of the two, numbers, and the underscore. You ought not perceive any spaces inside.

The identifier can't begin with a number

The identifier can't be a catchphrase and it should exclude one of the watchwords inside.

In the event that you defy one of these norms, the program will close on you and will demonstrate a language structure blunder. Likewise, you have to take a shot at making identifiers that are readable to human. While the identifier might be to the PC and get past without causing issues on the PC, a human is the person who will peruse the code to utilize it themselves. On the off chance that the human eye doesn't comprehend what you are writing in a specific spot, you could keep running into certain issues. A portion of the principles that you ought to pursue when making an identifier that will be meaningful to the human eye include:

The identifier ought to be clear—you should select name that will portray what is inside the variable or will depict what it does.

You ought to be cautious with utilizing condensings that aren't vital in light of the fact that these consistently make things that are troublesome.

While there are a great deal of ways that you can work out your code, you ought to be cautious and stick with one principle all through. For instance, both MyBestFriend and mybestfriend work in the coding scene, yet pick one that you like and do it the equivalent each time that you work in the program to maintain a strategic distance from perplexity. You can likewise include underscores into this or numbers, simply be cautious that you keep things reliable.

Flow of Control

When taking a shot at the Python language, you will work out the anstatements in a rundown position, much the same as you would when working out a shopping list. The PC will begin with the principal guidance before working through every one of them in the request that you make them appear on the rundown. So you should work out the controls that you need simply like you would for your shopping for food rundown to make sure that the PC is perusing it appropriately. The PC will just quit perusing this rundown once it has done the last guidance to finish. This is known as the progression of control.

This is a significant method to begin. You need to make sure that your progression of control is even and smooth for the PC to peruse. This will make it simpler to get the program to do what you might want without the same number of issues and guarantees that the PC program doesn't stall out, cause issues, or have something different turn out badly.

Semi-colons and Indentation

When you take a gander at a portion of the other programming languages, you will see that there are a great deal of wavy sections used to orchestrate the various squares of code or to start and end the announcements. This causes you to make sure to indent the code obstructs in these dialects to make the code simpler to peruse, despite the fact that the PC will have the option to peruse the various codes without the spaces fine and dandy.

This type of coding can make it extremely hard to peruse. You will see a ton of superfluous data that is required for the PC to peruse the code, yet can make it hard on the human eye to understand this. Python utilizes an alternate method for doing this, generally to help make it simpler on the human eye to peruse what you have. You are going to need to indent the code for this to work. A case of this is:

 # this function definition starts another square

def add_numbers (b, c): d= b + c

 # as is this one

return **d**

 # this function definition is the start of a new-block

if it is Snday

print (It's Wednesday!"

 # and this particular one is outside of this block

print ("Print this no matter what.")

In addition, there exist a lot of languages that will use a semicolon to indicate when an instruction ends.

In any case, Python however, you will utilize line finishes to tell the PC when a guidance will end. You'll have the option to utilize a semi-colon on the off chance that you have a couple of guidelines that are on a similar line, yet this is frequently viewed as inappropriate behavior inside the language.

Letter Case

Most scripts will treat capitalized and lowercase letters the equivalent, however Python is one of the main ones that will be case touchy. This implies the lower case and capitalized letters will be dealt with distinctively in the framework. Remember too that all the saved words will utilize lower case aside from None, False, and genuine.

These rudiments are going to make it simpler to begin on the Python programming. You have to set aside a touch of effort to experience the program so as to get acquainted with it. You won't have to turn into a specialist, however getting acquainted with a portion of the content mediator and a portion of different pieces of the program can make it simpler to utilize and you can figure out how the various catches will function even before you begin. Evaluate a couple of the models above first to enable you to begin.

Python attempts to keep things as essential as conceivable on the grounds that it comprehends that the greater part of its clients will be learners or the individuals who are sick of other complex dialects. As should be obvious here, and in the accompanying sections, there are straightforward directions that you will have the option to take care of forward to get the program to work a particular way. Concentrate these and you can make an incredible program without very as much work.

Remarks/comments in Python

There are a great deal of things that you can do in Python. It is one of the most intelligent alternatives that you will keep running into when beginning in programming and since it is so natural to utilize. In this part, we will set aside some effort to examine progressively about remarks and a portion of different parts of Python so you can begin and make your codes astonishing in a matter of seconds.

In Python programming a remark is one that will begin with the # sign and after that will proceed until you get as far as possible of the line. For instance:

 # There are going be just another comments

print("Hello, How are you doing?)

This would advise the PC to simply print "Hello, how are you doing?" All remarks are disregarded in the Python mediator since it is to a greater degree a commentary in the program to support the software engineer, or other people who may utilize the code, extraordinary things about the code. They are essentially there to state what the program should do and how it will function. It is more itemized and can be useful without hindering how the code functions.

You won't have to leave a remark on each line, exactly when it is required. In the event that the software engineer feels that something needs clarified better, they would place in a remark yet don't hope to see it everywhere. Python doesn't bolster any remarks that will go over a few lines so on the off chance that you have a more drawn out remark in the program, make sense of how to separate it into various lines with the # sign before each part.

Composing and Reading

A couple of projects will show the substance you need on the screen, or they can request certain data. You may need to start the program code by telling the peruser what your program is about. Assigning it a name or a title can make things less complex so the other coder grasps what is in the program and can pick the correct one for them.

The most ideal approach to get the correct data to show up is demonstrate a string strict that will incorporate the "print" work. For the individuals who don't have the foggiest idea, string literals are essentially lines of content that will be encompassed by certain statements, either a solitary or twofold statement. The type of statement that you use won't make any difference that much, yet on the off chance that you utilize one type in the start of the expression, you should utilize it toward the end. So if there are twofold statements toward the start of your expression, make sure that you stay aware of the twofold statements toward the end too.

When you need the PC to show a word or expression on the screen, you would essentially have "print" and afterward the expression after it. For instance, in the event that you need to depict.

"Hi, welcome!" you would do

Print("Welcome!")

This will make it so that "Welcome" pop up on your program for others to use. The print function will take up its very own line so you will see that in the wake of placing this in, the code will consequently put you on another line.

Probably you might want to have the guest do a specific activity, you can go with a similar sort of thought. For instance, say you need the individual to enter a particular number with the goal that they can traverse the code you would utilize the string:

second_number = input('put the second number in.')

When utilizing the input feature, you won't consequently observe it print on another line. The content will be set just after the brief. You will likewise need to change over the string into a number for the program to work. You don't have to have a particular parameter for this either. On the off chance that you do the accompanying alternative with simply the enclosures and nothing inside, you will get a similar outcome and in some cases makes it simpler.

Chapter 2: Files

Generally, you will utilize the print capacity to get a string to print to the screen. This is the default of the print work, however you can likewise utilize this equivalent capacity as a decent method to compose something onto a document. A genuine case of this is here:

with open('myfile.txt', 'v') as myfile: Print("Hello there!",file=myfile)

Presently this may resemble a basic condition, however there is a lot that is going on in the string over that you should watch out for. At the point when you opened up the myfile.txt to compose on and after that doled out it to the variable called myfile. At that point in the subsequent part, you wrote in Hello! To the record as another line and after that the w told the program that you may have the option to compose the progressions when the document is open.

Obviously, you don't need to utilize the print capacity to get it to take every necessary step that you need. The compose technique will frequently function admirably as well. For instance, you can supplant the print with compose like the model beneath to get very similar things.

with open('myfile.txt', 'v') as myfile: myfile.write("Hello there!")

So far, we have figured out how to print a string of words into the program and even how to spare them to a particular record. Notwithstanding those alternatives, you can utilize the read technique so as to open a particular document and afterward to peruse the data that is there. If perhaps that you might want to open and peruse a particular record, utilize this choice:

With open('myfile.txt', 'w') as my file:

data = my file. read ()

With this option, the program will be instructed to read up the files contents to a variable data. This can make it much easier to open up those programs that you might love to read later.

Built In Types

Your PC is equipped for handling a great deal of data including numbers and characters. The types of data that the Python program will utilize are known as types and the language will contain a wide range of types to help make things simpler. A portion of these incorporate string, whole numbers, and coasting point numbers. Software engineers can even characterize these various types utilizing classes.

Types will comprise of two separate parts. The initial segment is an area that will contain a conceivable arrangement of values and the subsequent part is a set that contains the potential activities. Both of these can be carried out on any worth. A case of this is on the off chance that you have a space that is a type of number; it can just contain whole numbers inside it including expansion, division, duplication, and subtraction.

One thing to note with this is Python is a progressively typed program. This implies there truly isn't a need to determine the types for the factors when you make it. Similar factors can be utilized to store the values of various types. Regardless of this, Python still needs you to have every one of the factors with a complete type. For instance, if the software engineer attempted to include a number to a string, the Python program would perceive this and demonstrate a mistake. It won't attempt to make sense of what you needed; rather it will simply exit easily.

Integers

If you need to utilize integers as a type, you have to keep them as entire numbers. These can be certain or negative numbers, insofar as there are no decimals with these numbers. In the event that you have a decimal point in the number, regardless of whether the number is 1.0, you should utilize it as a coasting point number.

Python can show these whole numbers in the "print" work, however just on the off chance that it is the sole contention.

Print(3)

Let's include two numbers together

Print(1+2)

Also, if that you are utilizing whole numbers, you won't have the option to put the two appropriate beside one another. This is mostly a result of how Python is a specifically language and won't remember them on the off chance that you join them together. Youmight want to put the number and the string together, you have to make sure that the number has transformed to string.

Operator Precedence

One thing that you have to monitor when you are working in Python is administrator priority. For instance, on the off chance that you have 1+2//3 Python could translate it as (1+2)//3 or 1+(2//3). Python has a strategy that will assist you with ordering the activity appropriately so you get the correct data to come up. For instance, with regards to whole number activity, Python is going to deal with everything that is sections first. At that point it will deal with the things that have**, at that point

*, and afterward/, then %, +, lastly - .

In the event that you are composing an articulation that has various tasks in it, you should remember those signs. This will disclose to Python how to experience the numbers with the goal that you can get the correct answers at the time. Remember that most number juggling administrators will be left acquainted so work it out that path for Python to peruse. The main special case is the ** include. For instance:

** is correct acquainted 2**3**4

will be assessed appropriate to left:

2**(3**4)

Strings

While a string may appear to be something confounded, in Python they are essentially a grouping of characters. They are getting down to business a similar path as a rundown does, yet they will contain more usefulness that is explicit to the content.

Designing strings can be a test with regards to working out your out your code. There are a few messages that won't be fixed string and once in a while there are values that are stored inside factors inside it. There is an approach to get this to work directly for string arranging. A case of this is:

Name = "Janet" Age = 24

Print("Hello! My name is %s." % name)

The images that have a % first are called placeholders. The factors that go into these positions will be set after the % in the request where they are put in the string. On the off chance that you are doing only a solitary string, you won't require a wrapper, yet on the off chance that you do have more than one of these, you have to put them into a tuple, with a () walling it in. The placeholder images will begin with various letters, depending for the most part on the variable type you are utilizing. For instance, the age will be a whole number by the name is a string. These factors will be changed over into the string before you can include them into the rest.

Escape Sequences

The escape sequence can be utilized as an approach to mean uncommon characters that can be difficult to type on your console. Moreover, they can be utilized to indicate characters that can be held for something different. For instance, utilizing and in the arrangement can befuddle the program so you may utilize the departure succession to supplant that like the accompanying model:

Print("This is a line. \nThis is a different line.")

Triple Quotes

We have invested a touch of energy discussing both single and twofold statements, however there are times when you may need to get the triple statement. This is utilized when you have to characterize an exacting that will traverse numerous lines or one that as of now has a great deal of statements in it. To do this, simply utilize a solitary and twofold together or three singles. A similar standard applies with the triple statement likewise with all the others. You should begin and close the expression with the equivalent trile quote.

Chapter 3: String Operations

One of the string tasks that you may utilize a great deal is a connection. This is utilized so as to join a couple of strings together and you will see it is there with the + image. There are a great deal of capacities that Python can assist you with and they will work with the strings to make an assortment of tasks. They will have some valuable choices that can do much more in the Pythons program

In Python program, strings are called changeless. This implies once you make the string, it isn't fit for being changed. You may need to dole out another important to a particular variable that exists on the off chance that you are hoping to make a few changes.

There is so much that you are able to learn about when it comes to getting started with Python. It may be a simple language, but you want to be able to learn how it works, how to write things down properly, and even how to leave a comment for others to understand when they are looking through the code. It may seem a bit intimidating in the beginning, but before too long, and with some practice, you will get it down and be writing your own code in no time.

The Assignment Sign

Take note that the = sign in the statement userAge = 0 has quite a number of meaning from the = sign we learned in Math. In python programming, the = sign is known as an assignment sign. It connotes that we are assigning the value which is on the right side of the = sign to the variable on the left. A great method to understand the statement userAge = 0 is to have the thought of it as the userAge <- 0.

The statements y = z and z = y . have very different meanings in programming

Confused? An example will likely clear this up.

Input the following code into your IDLE editor and save it up.

```
y = 5

z = 10

y = z

print ("y = ", y)

print ("z = ", z)
```

Now run the program. You should get this output:

```
y = 10

z = 10
```

Although our x has an initial value of 5 (declared on the first line), the third line y = z assigns the value of z to y (y <- z), hence changing the value of y to 10 while the value of z is still unchanged.

Next up, modify the program by changing ONLY ONE statement: Change the third line from y = z to z = y. Mathematically, y = z and z = y mean the same thing. However, this is not so when it comes to programming.

Run the second program. You will now get

y = 10

z = 10

You can notice that in this example, the y value remains as 10, but the value of z is changed to 10. This is because the statement z = y assigns the value of y to z (z <- y). z becomes 10 while y remains unchanged as 10.

Basic Operators

Other than relegating a variable an underlying value, we can likewise play out the standard scientific activities on factors. Essential administrators in Python incorporate +, - ,/, % and * which speak to expansion, subtraction, augmentation, division, floor division, modulus and exponent separately.

Example:

Suppose y = 10, z = 4 Addition: y + z = 7 Subtraction: y - z = 3 Multiplication: y*z = 10 Division: y/z = 4.10

Floor Division: y//z = 4 (rounds down the answer to the nearest whole number)

Modulus: y%z = 1 (gives the remainder when 10 is divided by 4) Exponent: y**z = 410 (10 to the power of 4)

More on Assignment Operators.

In addition to the = sign, there are a few more assignment operators in Python (and other programming languages). These include operators like +=, -= and *=.

Suppose we have the variable y, with an initial value of 10. If we want to increment y bz 4, we can write

y = y + 4

The program will first evaluate the eypression on the right (y + 4) and assign the answer to the left. So eventuallz the statement above becomes y <- 14.

Instead of writing y = y + 4, we can also write y += 4 to express the same meaning. The += sign is actually a shorthand that adds the assignment sign with the addition operator. Hence, y += 4 simply means y = y + 4.

Similarly, if we would love to do a subtraction, we can write y = y - 4 or y - = 4. The same thing works for all the 7 operators mentioned in the section above.

Chapter 4: Data Types in Python

In this chapter, we'll take a critical look at some basic data types in Python, categorically the integer, float and string. Moving forward, we'll explore the concept of type casting. Lastly, we'll talk about three more advanced data types in Python which are the list, tuple and dictionary.

Integers

Integers are those numbers without decimal parts, such as -6, -5, -2, 0, 2, 6 etc.

To declare an integer in Python programming, simply write variableName = initial value

Example:

userAge = 50, mobileNumber = 12398724

Float

Float is the name given to numbers that have decimal parts, such as 1.234, -0.023, 12.01.

To declare a float in Python, we will write variableName = initial value

Example:

userHeight. = 2.92, userWeight = 67.5

String

String also refers to text.

To declare a string, you might either utilize variableName = 'initial value' (single quotes) or variableName = "initial value" (double quotes)

Example:

userName = 'Peter', userSpouseName = "Janet", userAge

= '30'

In retrospect to our last example, because we used userAge = '30', userAge is a string. Otherwise, if you typed userAge = 30 (without quotes), userAge is known as the integer.

You can also combine different substrings by using the concatenate sign (+). For example, "Paul" + "Lee" is equivalent to the string "PaulLee".

Built-In String Functions

Python has many of built-in functions which are used to manipulate strings. A function is basically a block of reusable code that performs a certain task.

A good example of a function available in Python is the upper() method for strings. You use it for capitalizing all the letters in a string. For example, 'Paul'.upper() will give us the string "PAUL".

Type Casting In Python

Sometimes in python program, it is necessary for us to convert from one data type to another, such as from an integer to a string. This is known as type casting.

There are essentially 3 built in function in Python that enable us to perform type casting in python programming. These include the int(), float(), and str() functions.

The int() work in Python takes in a buoy or a proper string and changes over it to a number. To change over a buoy to a whole number, we can type int(5.712987). We'll have 5 as the outcome (anything after the decimal point is evacuated). To change a string to a whole number, we can type int ("4") and we'll get 4. Nonetheless, we can't type int ("Hello") or int ("4.22321"). We'll get a blunder in the two cases.

The buoy() work takes in a whole number or a suitable string and changes it to a buoy. For example, on the off chance that we type float(2) or float("2"), we'll get 2.0. In the event that we type float("2.09109"), we'll get 2.09109 which is a buoy and not a string since the quotes are expelled.

The str() work then again changes over a whole number or a buoy to a string. For example, on the off chance that we type str(2.1), we'll get "2.1".

Since we've secured the three essential data types in Python and their throwing, we should proceed onward to the further developed data types.

List

List alludes to an accumulation of data which are typically related. Rather than putting away these data as discrete factors, we can store them as a rundown. For example, assume our program needs to store the age of 5 clients. Rather than putting away them as user1Age, user2Age, user3Age, user4Age and user5Age, it makes more sense to store them as a rundown.

To pronounce a list, you compose listName = [initial values]. Note that we utilize square sections [ ] when proclaiming a rundown. Various values are isolated by a comma.

Model:

userAge = [21, 22, 23, 24, 25]

We can likewise pronounce a list/rundown without appointing any underlying values to it. We essentially compose listName = []. What we have now is an unfilled rundown without any things in it. We need to utilize the attach() strategy referenced beneath to add things to the rundown.

Individual values in the rundown are open by their lists, and records consistently start from ZERO, not 1. This is a typical practice in practically all programming dialects, for example, C and Java. Subsequently the primary worth has a list of 0, the following has a file of 1, etc. For example, userAge[0] = 21, userAge[1] = 22

On the other hand, you can get to the values of a rundown from the back. The last thing in the rundown has a record of - 1, the subsequent last has a file of - 2, etc. Subsequently, userAge[-1] = 25, userAge[-2] = 24.

You can allocate a rundown, or some portion of it, to a variable. On the off chance that you compose userAge2 = userAge, the variable userAge2 progresses toward becoming [21, 22, 23, 24, 25].

In the event that you compose userAge3 = userAge[2:4], you are relegating things with list 2 to list 4-1 from the rundown userAge to the rundown userAge3. As it were, userAge3 = [23, 24].

The documentation 2:4 is known as a cut. At whatever point we utilize the cut documentation in Python, the thing toward the beginning list is constantly included, however the thing toward the end is constantly prohibited. Henceforth the documentation 2:4 alludes to things from list 2 to list 4-1 (for example file 3), which is the reason userAge3 = [23, 24] and not [23, 24, 25].

The cut documentation incorporates a third number known as the stepper. On the off chance that we compose userAge4 = userAge[1:5:2], we will get a sub rundown comprising of consistently number from file 1 to file 5-1 in light of the fact that the stepper is 2. Thus, userAge4 = [22, 24].

Furthermore, cut documentations have helpful defaults. The default for the primary number is zero, and the default for the subsequent number is size of the rundown being cut. For example, userAge[:4] gives you esteems from file 0 to file 4-1 while userAge[1:] gives you esteems from list 1 to file 5-1 (since the size of userAge is 5, for example userAge has 5 things).

To change things in a rundown, we compose listName[index of thing to be modified] = new worth. For example, on the off chance that you need to adjust the subsequent thing, you compose userAge[1] = 5. Your rundown progresses toward becoming userAge = [21, 5, 23, 24, 25]

To include things, you utilize the attach() work. For example, in the event that you use userAge.append(99), you add the worth 99 as far as possible of the rundown. Your rundown is presently userAge = [21, 5, 23, 24, 25, 99]

To expel things, you compose del listName[index of thing to be deleted]. For example, in the event that you use del userAge[2], your rundown presently progresses toward becoming userAge = [21, 5, 24, 25, 99] (the third thing is erased).

To fully appreciate the usefulness of lists, run the following code.

list elements can include different types:

```python
myList = [1, 2, 3, 4, 5, "Hello"]

#print the whole list.

print(myList)

#You'll have [1, 2, 3, 4, 5, "Hello"]

#print the third object(remember: Indexes start at zero).

print(myList[2])

#It will print 3

#print the last item.

print(myList[-1])

#It will print "Hello"

#assign myList (index 1 to 4) to myList2, then print myList2

myList2 = myList[1:4]

print (myList2)

#It will print [2, 3, 4, 5]

#edit the 2nd item in myList, then print the updated list

myList[1] = 20

print(myList)

#It will print [1, 20, 3, 4, 5, 'Hello']

#append a new string to myList and print the new list

myList.append("How are you")

print(myList)

#It will print [1, 20, 3, 4, 5, 'Hello', 'How are you']
```

```python
#delete the 6th item from myList, then print the list

del

myList[5]

print(myList)

#It will print [1, 20, 3, 4, 5, 'How are you']
```

Tuple

Tuples are much the same as lists, however you can't alter their qualities. The underlying qualities are the qualities that will remain for the remainder of the program. A Dictionary where tuples are helpful is the point at which your program has to cache the names of the months of the year.

To pronounce a tuple, you compose tupleName = (starting qualities). Notice that we use round sections ( ) when announcing a tuple. Numerous qualities are isolated by a comma.

Dictionary:

monthsOfYear = ("Jan", "Feb", "March", "Apr", "May",

"Jun", "Jul", "Aug", "Sep", "Oct", "Nov", "Dec")

You get to the individual estimations of a tuple utilizing their records, much the same as with a list.

Subsequently, monthsOfYear[0] = "Jan", monthsOfYear[-1] = "Dec".

Dictionary

Dictionary is an accumulation of related information PAIRS. For example, in the event that we need to store the username and age of 5 clients, we can store them in a dictionary.

To proclaim a dictionary, you compose dictionaryName = {dictionary key : data}, with the necessity that dictionary keys must be special (inside one dictionary). Along these lines, it is beyond the realm of imagination to expect to proclaim a dictionary like this

myDictionary = {"Peter":38, "John":51, "Peter":13}.

The explanation is that "Subside" is utilized as the dictionary key twice. Note that we utilize wavy sections { } when announcing a dictionary. Various sets are isolated by a comma.

Dictionary:

userNameAndAge = {"Paul":38, "John":51, "Alley":13, "Alvin":"Not Available"}

You can likewise proclaim a dictionary utilizing the dict( ) strategy. To announce the userNameAndAge dictionary above, you compose

userNameAndAge = dict(Paul= 38, John = 51, Alley = 13, Alvin = "Not Available")

When you utilisize this strategy to proclaim a dictionary, you utilize round sections ( ) rather than wavy sections { } and you don't put quotes for the dictionary keys.

To arrive at the individual things in the dictionary, we utilize the dictionary key, which is the primary incentive in the {dictionary key : data} pair. For example, to get John's age, you input userNameAndAge["John"].

You'll get the worth 51.

To change things in a dictionary, we compose dictionaryName[dictionary key of thing to be modified] = new information.

For example, to change the "John":51 pair, we compose userNameAndAge["John"] = 21. Our dictionary presently progresses toward becoming userNameAndAge = {"Paul":38, "John":21, "Alley":13, "Alvin":"Not Available"}.

It is additionally conceivable to announce a dictionary without doling out any underlying qualities to it. We basically compose dictionaryName = { }. What we have now is an unfilled dictionary without any things in it.

To add things to a dictionary, we compose dictionaryName[dictionary key] = information. For example, on the off chance that we need to include "Joe":40 to our dictionary, we compose userNameAndAge["Joe"] = 40. Our dictionary presently progresses toward becoming userNameAndAge = {"Peter":38, "John":21, "Alex":13, "Alvin":"Not Available", "Joe":40}

To expel things from a dictionary, we compose del dictionaryName[dictionary key]. For example, to expel the "Alex":13 pair, we compose del userNameAndAge["Alley"]. Our dictionary currently moves toward becoming userNameAndAge = {"Peter":38, "John":21, "Alvin":"Not Available", "Joe":40}

Run the accompanying system to see all these in real life.

#declaring the dictionary, dictionary keys and information can be of various information kinds

myDict = {"One":1.35, 4.5:"Two Point Five", 3:"+", 7.9:3}

#print the whole dictionary.

print(myDict)

#You'll get {4.5: 'Two Point Five', 3: '+', 'One': 1.35, 7.9: 3}

#Note the fact that things in a dictionary are not put away in a similar request as the manner in which you announce them.

```python
#print the thing with key = "One". print(myDict["One"])

#You'll get 1.35

#print the thing with key = 7.9. print(myDict[7.9])

#You'll get 2

#modify the thing with key = 2.5 and print the refreshed dictionary

myDict[2.5] = "Over two" print(myDict)

#You'll get {2.5: 'Over two', 3: '+', 'One': 1.35, 7.9: 2}

#add another thing and print the refreshed dictionary myDict["New item"] =
"I'm new"

print(myDict)

#You'll get {'New thing': 'I'm new', 2.5: 'Over two', 3: '+', 'One': 1.35, 7.9: 2}

#remove the thing with key = "One" and print the refreshed dictionary

del myDict["One"]

print(myDict)
```

Chapter 5: Making Python Programming More Interactive

Since we've secured the fundamentals of variables, let us compose a program that utilizes them. We'll return to the "Welcome World" program prior yet this time we'll make it intuitive. Rather than trying to say hi to the world, we need the world to know our names and ages as well. So as to do that, our program should have the option to provoke us for data and show them on the screen.

Two inherent capacities can do that for us: information() and print(). For the time being, how about we type the accompanying project in IDLE. Spare it and run it.

myName = input("Please input your Name: ")

myAge = input("Please enter your age also: ")

You will print (hi Every one, my name is, myName, "and I am", myAge, "years old.")

The program should incite you for your name.

If it's not too much stress enter your name:

Assumed you entered James. Presently press Enter and it'll incite you for your age.

Shouldn't something be said about your age:

Let's assume you entered in 20. Presently press Enter once more. You ought to get the accompanying proclamation:

Hi World, my name is James and I am 20 years of age.

Input ()

In the model above, we used the input() work twice to get the user's name and age.

myName = input("Kindly input your first name: ")

The string "Please enter your first name: " is the concise that will be showed up on the screen to hand-off rules to the customer. After the customer enters the significant information, this information is taken care of as a string in the variable myName. The accompanying input clarification prompts the customer for his age and stores the information as a string in the variable myAge.

The input() work shifts hardly in Python 2 and Python 3. In Python 2, if you have to recognize customer input as a string, you have to use the raw_input() work.

Print()

The print() work is used to demonstrate information to customers. It recognizes at any rate zero explanations as parameters, disengaged by commas.

In the declaration underneath, we passed 5 parameters to the print() work. Okay have the option to remember them?

print ("Hi Everyone, my name is", myName, "and I am", myAge, "years old.")

The first is the string "Greetings World, my name is" Coming up next is the variable myName declared using the input limit previously. Sought after is the string "and I am", trailed by the variable myAge finally the string "years old.".

Note that we don't use cites when insinuating the elements myName and myAge. If you use cites, you'll get the yield

Hi Everyone, my name is myName and I am myAge years old.

Or maybe, which is plainly not what we need.

Another way to deal with print a declaration with variables is to use the % formatter. To achieve a comparative yield as the chief print clarification above, we can create

print ("Hi World". Your name is #s and you are years old #s (my name, my age))

By then, to print a comparable clarification going by the association() technique, we form

print ("Hi Everyone, my name is {} and I am {} years old".format(my name, myage))

The print() work is another limit that differentiations in Python 2 and Python 3. You form it without segments in Python 2, like this:

print 'Hello World', my name is " + myName + " and I am " + myAge + " years old"

Triple Quotes

In case you need to demonstrate a long message, you can use the triple-quote picture (''' or """) to navigate your message over various lines. For instance, print ('''Hello World.

My name is Fabian and I am 15 years old.''') will give you

Greetings World.

My name is Fabian and I am 15 years old.

This fabricates the weightiness of your text.

Escape Chars

Sometimes we may need to print some specific chars like a tab or a newline.

In this case, you need to use the \ (backslash) character to escape characters that will, otherwise, have a different meaning.

For example to print a tab, we have to input the backslash character before the letter t, like this: \t. Without the addition of \ character, the letter t will be printed. With it, a tab is printed.

Henceforth, on the off chance that you type print ('Hello\tWorld'), you'll get Hello World

Other generally discovered employments of the oblique punctuation line character are demonstrated as follows.

>>> demonstrates the direction and the accompanying lines demonstrate the yield.

\n (Prints a newline)

>>> print ('Hello\nWorld') Hello

World

\\ (Prints the oblique punctuation line character itself)

>>> print ('\\')

\' (Prints twofold statement, so that that the twofold statement doesn't suggest the finish of the string)

>>> print ('I am 4'8\" tall") I am 4'8"

\' (Print single quote, in such a way that the single quote does not indicate the end of the string)

>>> print ('I am 4\'8" tall') I am 4'8" tall

In the event that you don't need characters gone before by the \ character to be translated as exceptional characters, you can utilize crude strings by including a r before the primary statement. For instance, on if perhaps that you don't need \t to be translated as a tab, you should type print (r'Hello\tWorld'). You will get Hello\tWorld as the result.

Chapter 6: Making Choices

Congratulations, this is likely the most interesting chapter.

I hope you've liked the course so far. Now, ian this chapter, we'll understand how to make your software smarter, capable of making decisions.

Specifically, we'll be learning the if statement, the for loop and the while loop. These are known as control flow tools because they control the flow. In addition, we'll also take a look at the try & except statements that defines what the program should do in case an error occurs.

Anyway, before we dig into these tools, we have to learn condition statements.

Conditional Statements

Any control flow code involves evaluating a condition statement and behaving accordingly. The software will proceed depending on whether the condition is met or not.

The most common statement is the comparison statement.

If we want to check if two variables have the same value, we use the == sign (double =). For example, if your statement is x == y, you are asking the code to check if the value of x equals the value of y. If they are the same, the condition is met, then the statement will be true. Otherwise, the command will evaluate to false.

Other comparison symbols include != (not equals), < (smaller than), > (greater than), <= (smaller than or equals to) and >= (bigger than or equals to). The list below shows how these symbols can be used and gives examples of statements that will evaluate to True.

Not equals: 5 != 2

Greater than: 5>2

Smaller than: 2<5

Greater than or equals to: 5>=2 5>=5

Smaller than or equals to: 2 <= 5. 2 <= 2

We additionally have three logical operators, and, or, not excessively are helpful in the event that we need to consolidate numerous conditions.

The and administrator/operator returns True if all conditions are met. Else it will return False. For example, the announcement 5==5 and 2>1 will return True since the two conditions are True.

The or administrator will return True if at any rate 1 condition is met. Else it will return False. The announcement 5 > 2 or 7 > 10 or 3 == 2 will return True since the main condition 5>2 is True.

Here, the not operator returns True when the condition immediately after the not keyword is false. Else it will return False. Not 2>5 statement will return True since 2 is not greater than 5.

If Statement

The if statement is known to be one of the most broadly utilized control stream statements. It enables the program to assess if a specific condition is met, and to play out the proper activity dependent on the consequence of the assessment. The sythesis of an if statement is as per the following:

if condition 1 is met: do An elif condition 2 is met: do B elif condition 3 is met: do C elif condition 4 is met: do D else:

do E

elif means "else if" and you can have the same number of elif statements as you like.

If you've coded in different dialects like C or Java previously, you might be amazed to see that no enclosures ( ) are required in Python after the if, elif and else watchword. What's more, Python doesn't use wavy { } sections to characterize the start and end of the if statement. Or maybe, Python utilizes space. Anything indented is treated as a square of code that will be executed if the condition assesses to genuine.

To completely see how the if statement functions, fire up IDLE and key in the accompanying code.

userInput = input('Enter 1 or 2: ')

if userInput == "1": print ("Hello World,")

print ("How are you?")

elif userInput == "2": print ("Python Rocks!")

print ("I adore Python") else:

print ("You didn't enter a legitimate number")

The program first prompts the client for an info utilizing the information work. The outcome is put away in the userInput variable as a string.

Next the statement if userInput == "1": contrasts the userInput variable and the string "1". If the worth put away in userInput is "1", the program will execute all statements that are indented until the space closes. In this model, it'll print "Hi World", at that point it will be pursued "How are you?"

On the other hand, if the worth put away in userInput is "2", the program will print "Python is Cool", trailed by "I adore Python".

For every single other worth, the program will print "You didn't enter a substantial number".

Run the program multiple times, enter 1, 2 and 3 individually for each run. You'll get the ouput below:

Enter 1 or 2:1 Hello World!, how are you?

Enter 1 or 2: 2 Python is Cool!I adore Python

Enter 1 or 2: 3

You didn't enter a valid number

Inline If

The inline if statement is a less complex type of an if statement and is increasingly helpful if you just need to play out a straightforward undertaking. The linguistic structure is:

Perform Task An if condition is genuine else do Task B

For example,

num1 = 12 if myInt==10 else 13

This statement allots 12 to num1 (Task An) if myInt equivalents to 10. Else it doles out 13 to num1 (Task B).

Another model is

print ("This is task An" if myInt == 10 else "This is task B")

This statement gives "This is task A" (Task An) if myInt equivalents to 10. Else it shows "This is task B" (Task B).

For Loop

Next, let us discuss the for loop. The for loop executes a square of code over and over until the condition in the for explanation is never again substantial.

Looping through an iterable

In Python, an iterable is known to be whatever can be looped over, for example, a string, list or tuple. The linguistic structure for looping through an iterable is as per the following:

for an in iterable: print (a)

Model:

pets = ['cats', 'hounds', 'bunnies', 'hamsters'] for myPets in pets:

print (myPets)

In the program above, we initially announce the rundown pets and give it the individuals 'felines', 'hounds', 'hares' and 'hamsters'. Next the announcement for myPets in pets: loops through the pets list and appoints every part in the rundown to the variable myPets.

The first run through the program goes through the for loop, it doles out 'felines' to the variable myPets. The announcement print (myPets) at that point prints the worth 'felines'. The second time the projects loops through the for articulation, it puts the worth 'hounds' to myPets and prints the worth 'hounds'. The program keeps looping through the rundown until the finish of the rundown is come to.

In the event that you run the program, you'll get

felines

hounds

bunnies hamsters

We can likewise show the list of the individuals in the rundown. To do that, we utilize the list() work.

for record, myPets in enumerate(pets): print (file, myPets)

This will give us the yield

0 cats

1 dogs

2 rabbits

3 hamster

The following model tells the best way to loop through a string.

message = 'Hi'

for I in message: print (I)

The ouput we have :

H

e

l

l

o

Looping through an arrangement of numbers

To loop through an arrangement of numbers, the inherent range() work proves to be useful. The range() work creates a rundown of numbers and has the language structure extend (start, end, step).

In the event that start isn't given, the numbers created will begin from zero.

Note: A helpful hint to recollect here is that in Python (and most programming dialects), except if generally expressed, we generally start from zero.

For example, the file of a rundown and a tuple begins from zero. When utilizing the format() technique for strings, the places of parameters start from zero.

When utilizing the range() work, if start isn't given, the numbers produced start from zero.

On the off chance that progression isn't given, a rundown of back to back numbers will be created (for example step = 1). The end worth must be given. In any case, one strange thing about the range() work is that the given end worth is never part of the produced rundown.

For example,

range(5) will create the rundown [0, 1, 2, 3, 4]

range(3, 10) will create [3, 4, 5, 6, 7, 8, 9]

range(4, 10, 2) will create [4, 6, 8]

To perceive how the range() work works in a for articulation, take a stab at running the accompanying line of code:

for i in range(5): print (i)

You should get

0

1

2

3

4

While Loop

The following control stream statement we are going to take a gander at is the while loop. Like the name recommends, a while loop over and again executes guidelines inside the loop while a specific condition stays legitimate. The syntax of this statement is the following:

while condition is valid: do A

More often than not when utilizing a while loop, we have to initially proclaim a variable to work as a loop counter. Allows simply call this variable counter. The condition in the while statement will assess the estimation of counter to decide whether it littler (or more prominent) than a specific worth. On the off chance that it is, the loop will be executed. How about we take a gander at an example program.

counter = 6

while counter > 1:

print ('Counter' = 'counter') counter = counter -1

If you run the program, you'll get the following output

Counter

=

6

Counter

=

5

Counter

=

4

Counter

=

3

Counter

=

2

From the start look, a while statement appears to have the least difficult sentence structure and ought to be the most straightforward to utilize. Notwithstanding, one must be cautious when utilizing while loops because of the threat of limitless loops. In the program above notice that we have the line counter = counter - 1? This line is vital. It diminishes the estimation of counter by 1 and doles out this new incentive back to counter, overwriting the first worth.

We need to bring down the estimation of counter by 1 with the goal that the loop condition while counter > 0 will at long last assess to False. In the event that we forget to do that, the loop will continue running unendingly bringing about a vast loop. In the event that you need to encounter this direct, simply erase the line counter = counter - 1 and have a go at running the program once more. Counter = 5 will continue printing by the program until you by one way or another slaughter the program. This is certainly not a decent encounter particularly on the off chance that you have an enormous program and you have no clue which code portion is causing the boundless loop.

Break

When working with loops, once in a while you might need to leave the whole loop when a specific condition is met. To do that, we utilize the break catchphrase.

Run the accompanying project to perceive how it functions.

j = 0

for I in range(5): j = j + 2

print ('I = ', I, ', j = ', j) if j == 6: break

We ought to get the accompanying yield.

i

=

0

,

j

=

2

i

=

1

,

j

=

4

i

=

2

,

j

=

6

Without the break keyword, the program ideally loops from i = 0 to i = 4 owing to the fact that we used the function range(5). However with the addition of the break keyword, the program closes rashly at I = 2. This is on the grounds that when I = 2, j arrives at the estimation of 6 and the break catchphrase makes the loop end.

In the model above, observe that we used an if statement inside a for loop. It is very expected of us to 'blend and-match' different control devices in programming, for example, utilizing a while loop inside an if statement or utilizing a for loop inside a while loop. This is known as a nested control statement.

Try, Except

The last control statement we'll investigate in this book is the attempt, with the exception of statement. This statement controls how the program continues when a blunder happens. The sentence structure is as per the following:

attempt:

accomplish something with the exception of:

accomplish something different when a blunder happens

For example, take a stab at running the program beneath

attempt:

answer =12/0 print (answer)

but:

print ("A blunder happened")

When you execute the program, you will ll see the message "A blunder happened". This is on the grounds that when the program attempts to execute the statement answer =12/0 in the attempt hinder, a mistake happens since you can't separate a number by zero. The staying of the attempt square is disregarded and the statement in the aside from square is executed.

On the off chance that you need to show progressively explicit mistake messages to your clients relying upon the blunder, you can determine the blunder type after the aside from catchphrase. Have a go at running the program underneath.

attempt:

userInput1 = int(input("Please enter the number: ")) userInput2 = int(input("Please enter another number: ")) answer =userInput1/userInput2

print ("The appropriate response is ", answer) myFile = open("missing.txt", 'r')
with the exception of ValueError:

print ("Error: You didn't enter a number") with the exception of
ZeroDivisionError: print ("Error: Cannot isolate by zero") aside from
Exception as e:

print ("Unknown mistake: ", e)

The rundown beneath demonstrates the different yields for various client
inputs. >>> signifies the client info and => indicates the yield.

>>> Please enter a number: m => Error: You didn't enter a number

Reason: User entered a string which can't be thrown into a whole number. This
is a ValueError. Henceforth, the statement in the aside from ValueError square
is shown.

>>> Please enter a number: 12

>>> Please enter another number: 0

=> Error: Cannot separate by zero

Reason: userInput2 = 0. Since we can't partition a number by zero, this is a
ZeroDivisionError. The statement in the aside from ZeroDivisionError square
is shown.

>>> Please enter a number: 12

>>> Please enter another number: 3

=> The appropriate response is 4.0

=> Unknown blunder: [Errno 2] No such record or index: 'missing.txt'

Reason: User enters worthy qualities and the line print ("The appropriate
response is ", answer) executes accurately. Nonetheless, the following line raises
a mistake as missing.txt isn't found. Since this isn't a ValueError or a
ZeroDivisionError, the last aside from square is executed.

ValueError and ZeroDivisionError are two of the numerous pre-characterized blunder types in Python. ValueError is brought when a developed in activity or capacity gets a parameter that has the correct kind however a wrong worth. ZeroDivisionError is raised when the program attempts to isolate by zero. Other regular mistakes in Python incorporate

IOError

Raised when an I/O activity/operation, (for example, the inherent open() work) falls flat for an I/O-related explanation, e.g., "document not found".

ImportError:

Raised when an import statement neglects to discover the module definition IndexError:

Raised when a grouping (for example string, list, tuple) file is out of range.

KeyError:

Raised when a lexicon key isn't found.

NameError:

Raised when a nearby or worldwide name isn't found.

TypeError:

Raised when an activity or capacity is applied to an object of unseemly kind.

For a total rundown of all the blunder types in Python, you can allude to https://docs.python.org/3/library/exceptions.html.

Python likewise accompanies pre-characterized mistake messages for every one of the various sorts of blunders. In the event that you need to show the message, you utilize the as watchword after the mistake type. For example, to show the default ValueError message, you compose:

with the exception of ValueError as e: print (e)

e is the variable name relegated to the mistake. You can give it some different names, however it is regular practice to utilize e. The last with the exception of statement in our program

but Exception as e:

print ("Unknown mistake: ", e) is a case of utilizing the pre-characterized mistake message. It fills in as a last endeavor to get any unexpected mistakes.

Chapter 7: Sets

A set type is **a group** of unique elements. Although a set itself is mutable, its elements must be immutable. Sets are used to carry out math operations involving sets such as intersection, union, or symmetric difference.

Creating a Set

You can create a set by enclosing all elements in curly braces {} or by using set(), one of Python's built-in functions. A set can hold items of different data types such as float, tuple, string, or integer. It cannot, however, hold a mutable element such as a dictionary, list, or set. Sets can hold any number of items. A comma is used to separate items from each other.

An example of s set of integers:

>>>my_set = {1, 4, 6, 8, 9, 10}

An example of a set of strings:

>>>my_set = {'a', 'e', 'i', 'o', 'u'}

An example of a set of mixed data types:

>>> my_set = {5.0, "Python", (5, 4, 2), 6}

An example of a set created from a list:

>>>set([5,4,3, 1])

{1, 3, 4, 5}

>>>

A set's elements cannot have a duplicate. When you create a set, Python evaluates if there are duplicates and drops the duplicate item.

Example #1:

>>> my_set = {'apple', 'peach', 'grape', 'apple', 'strawberry', 'grape'}

>>>my_set

{'peach', 'grape', 'apple', 'strawberry'}

>>>

Example #2:

```
>>>{1, 3, 5, 9, 1, 4, 3}
{1, 3, 4, 5, 9}
>>>
>>>set(['a', 'c', 'd', 'a', 'g', 'h', 'd'])
{'a', 'c', 'h', 'g', 'd'}
>>>
```

To create an empty set, you will have to use the set() function without an argument. You cannot use empty curly braces as this is the syntax for creating an empty dictionary.

```
>>> my_set = set()
>>>type(my_set)
<class 'set'>
>>>
```

Changing Elements on a Set

Sets are mutable so you can change their elements. Because sets are unordered, you cannot access or change an item or items through indexing or slicing like what you did earlier with strings and lists. You can, however, change the elements of a set with the methods **add()** or **update()**. The method add() appends a single element to a set while update() adds multiple elements. Strings, lists, tuples, or other sets can be used as argument when you use the update() method.

Example #1:

```
>>> my_set = {2, 4, 6, 8, 10}

>>> my_set.add(12)

>>> my_set

{2, 4, 6, 8, 10, 12}

>>>
```

Example #2:

```
>>> my_set = {2, 4, 6, 8, 10}

>>> my_set.update([14, 16, 18, 20])

>>> my_set

{2,4,6,8,10,12,14,16,18,20}

>>>
```

Example #3:

```
>>> my_set = {2, 4, 6, 8, 10}
```

```
>>> my_set.update('a', 'b')
>>> my_set
{2, 'a', 4, 6, 8, 10, 'b'}
>>>
```

Removing Set Elements

The **remove()** and **discard()** methods can be used to remove a specific item from a set. The only difference between the methods is their response to a non-existent argument. The use of the remove() method raises an error when the item given as argument does not exist. With discard(), the set simply remains unchanged.

Example #1:

```
>>> my_set = {'a', 'b', 'c', 'd', 'e', 'f', 'g'}

>>> my_set.discard('c')

>>> my_set

{'b', 'e', 'f', 'g', 'a', 'd'}

>>>
```

Example #2:

```
>>> my_set = {'a', 'b', 'c', 'd', 'e', 'f', 'g'}

>>> my_set.remove('f')

>>> my_set

{'e', 'd', 'b', 'c', 'a', 'g'}

>>>
```

Here is how Python responds when you use discard() with an item which is not foundon the set:

```
>>> my_set = {'a', 'b', 'c', 'd', 'e', 'f', 'g'}

>>> my_set.discard('x')

>>> my_set
```

{'g', 'd', 'e', 'c', 'a', 'f', 'b'}

>>>

The elements on the set were unchanged and no error was raised.

On the other hand, remove() will raise a Key Error if the item given as an argument is non-existent:

>>> my_set = {'a', 'b', 'c', 'd', 'e', 'f', 'g'}

>>> my_set.remove('x')

Traceback (most recent call last):

File "<pyshell#21>", line 1, in <module> my_set.remove('x')

KeyError: 'x'

>>>

The **pop()** method is likewise used to remove and return an item on a set. Since the **set is unordered**, you cannot possibly control which item will be popped. Selection is arbitrary.

>>> my_set = {'a', 'e', 'i', 'o', 'u'}

>>> my_set.pop()

'o'

>>> my_set

{'e', 'a', 'i', 'u'}

>>>

Now you can use the **clear()** method to remove all elements on a set.

>>> my_set = {'a', 'e', 'i', 'o', 'u'}

>>> my_set.clear()

```
>>> my_set set()

>>>
```

Set Operations

You can utilize sets to perform various set operations. To do this, you will use different Python operators or methods.

Set Union

A union of two sets refers to a set that contains all elements from the given sets. You can use the | **operator** or the **union()** method to perform the operation. The result is a combination of all elements which are returned in an **ascending order.**

Example with the | operator:

>>> x = {1,3,5,7,9,11,13}

>>> y = {2,4,6,8,10,12,14}

>>> x | y{1,2,3,4,5,6,7,8,9,10,11,12,13,14}

>>>

Example with the union() method:

>>> x = {1,3,5,7,9,11,13}

>>> y = {2,4,6,8,10,12,14}

>>> x.union(y)

{1,2,3,4,5,6,7,8,9,10,11,12,13,14}

>>>

Or

>>> x = {1,3,5,7,9,11,13}

```
>>> y = {2,4,6,8,10,12,14}

>>> y.union(X)

{1,2,3,4,5,6,7,8,9,10,11,12,13,14}

>>>
```

Set Intersection

The intersection of two different sets refers to the **set of common elements between them**. It is performed with either the **& operator** or the **intersection() method**. Both return a set with elements that are arranged in **ascending order**:

Example with the & operator:

```
>>> x = {1, 3, 5, 7, 2, 4, 6}

>>> y = {2, 4, 5, 7, 2, 0, 9}

>>> x & y

{2, 4, 5, 7}

>>>
```

Example with the intersection() method:

```
>>> x = {1, 3, 5, 7, 2, 4, 6}

>>> y = {2, 4, 5, 7, 2, 0, 9}

>>> x.intersection(y)

{2, 4, 5, 7}

>>> y.intersection(x)

{2, 4, 5, 7}

>>>
```

Set Difference

Set difference refers to a set of elements that are found in one set but not in the other set. For instance, the difference of X and Y (X – Y) is a set of elements that can be found in X but not in Y. Conversely, the difference of Y and X (Y – X) is a set of elements that are found in Y but not in X. The set difference operation is performed with either the **– operator** or the **difference() method**.

Examples with the - operator:

```
>>> x = {1, 2, 3, 5, 7, 9}
>>> y = {2, 8, 9, 5, 2, 1}
>>> x - y
{3, 7}
>>> y - x
{8}
>>>
```

Examples with the difference() method:

```
>>> x = {1, 2, 3, 5, 7, 9}
>>> y = {2, 8, 9, 5, 2, 1}
>>> x.difference(y)
{3, 7}
>>> y.difference(x)
{8}
>>>
```

Set Symmetric Difference

The symmetric difference between two sets refers to the set of elements that are not common in both sets. It is performed with either the ^ **operator** or the **symmetric_difference() method**.

Example with the ^ operator:

>>> a = {1, 3, 5, 4, 6, 8}

>>> b = {5, 2, 6, 1, 8, 10}

>>> a ^ b

{2, 3, 4, 10}

>>>

Examples with the symmetric_difference() method:

>>> a = {1, 3, 5, 4, 6, 8}

>>> b = {5, 2, 6, 1, 8, 10}

>>> a.symmetric_difference(b)

{2, 3, 4, 10}

>>> b.symmetric_difference(a)

{2, 3, 4, 10}

>>>

Set Membership Test

The **membership test operators**(the "in" and "not in" operators) can be used to test the existence or non-existence of an item on a set.

For example:

```
>>> my_set = {'land', 'sea', 'air', 'ocean', 'river'}

>>> 'sea' in my_set True

>>> 'river' not in my_set False

>>>
```

Using Built-in Functions with Set

There are several Python functions that are often used with set to carry out various tasks.

Len()

Returns the number of elements on a set.

>>>my_set = {1, 'a', 2, 'b', 3, 'c'}

>>>len(my_set) 6

>>>

Max()

Returns the largest element on a set.

>>>my_set = {1,2,3,4,5}

>>>max(my_set) 5

>>>

On a set of strings, max() returns the last item alphabetical-wise.

>>> b = {'a', 'b', 'c', 'd', 'e'}

>>>max(b) 'e'

>>>

Min()

Returns the smallest element on a set.

>>> a = {2, 1, 5, 8, 9, 20}

>>>min(a) 1

>>>

>>> b = {'a', 'b', 'c', 'd', 'e'}

>>>min(b) 'a'

>>>

Sorted()

Returns a sorted list of set elements but does not actually sort the set.

Chapter 8: Functions and Modules

Earlier in this book, we've briefly mentioned functions and modules. In this chapter, we will look at them in detail. Once again, all programming languages come with built-in codes that we can utilize to make our lives easier as programmers. These codes usually are made up of pre-written classes, variables and functions for performing certain common tasks and are saved in files known as modules. Let's first look at functions.

What are Functions?

Functions can be simply defined pre-written codes that perform a certain task. For an analogy, think of the mathematical functions available in MS Excel. To add numbers, we can use the sum() function and type sum(A1:A5) instead of typing A1+A2+A3+A4+A5.

Depending on the way function is written, whether it is part of a class (a class is a concept in object-oriented programming which we be discussed in advanced book) and how do you import it, we can call a function by simply typing the name of the function or by using the dot notation. Some functions require us to transfer data in for them to perform their tasks. These data are known as parameters and we pass them to the function by enclosing their values in parenthesis ( ) separated by commas.

For example, to utilize the print() function for displaying text on the screen, we will call it by typing print("Hello World") where print is the name of the function and "Hello World" is the parameter.

On the opposite hand, to use the change() function for manipulating text strings, we've get to type 'Hello World'.replace("World", "Universe") , here change is the name of the function and "World" and "Universe" are the parameters. The string before the dot (i.e. 'Hello World') is will be changed as a string. Hence, 'Hello World' will be turned to 'Hello Universe'.

Defining Your Own Functions

We can define our personal functions in Python to reuse them throughout the program. The step for defining a function is as below:

def functionName(parameters): code detailing what the function should do return [expression]

There are two keywords here, def and return.

def tells the program that the indented code from the next line onwards is part of the function. return is that keyword that we tend to return an answer from the function. There is possibility of more than one return statements in a function. However, once the function carries out a return statement, the function will exit. If your function does not require to return any value, you can leave out the return statement. Instead, you can just write return or return None.

Let us now define our first function. Suppose we want to determine if a given number is a prime number. Here's how we can define the function using the modulus (%) operator.

def checkIfPrime (numberToCheck): for x in range(2, numberToCheck): if (numberToCheck%x == 0):

return False return True

In the above function, lines 2 and 3 uses a for loop to divide the given parameter numberToCheck by all numbers from 2 to numberToCheck

- 1 to determine if the remainder is zero. If the remainder is zero, numberToCheck is not a prime number. Line 4 will give back False and the function will exit.

If through last iteration of the for loop, none of the division has a remainder of zero, the function will reach Line 5, and return True. Then, the function will then exit.

To use this function, we type checkIfPrime(13) and assign it to a variable like this

answer = checkIfPrime(13)

In this condition we are passing in 13 as the parameter. We can go ahead to print the answer by typing print(answer). We'll get the output: True.

Variable Scope

A very important concept to understand when defining a function is the concept of variable scope. Variables that defined inside of a function are treated differently from variables defined outside of it. There are two main differences.

Firstly, any variable declared <u>inside </u>a function is only accessible within the function. These are known as local variables. Any variable that is declared outside a function is known as a global variable and is accessible anywhere in the program.

To understand this, try the code below:

message1 = "Global Variable"

def myFunction():

print("\nINSIDE THE FUNCTION") #Global variables are accessible inside a function print (message1)

#Declaring a local variable message2 = "Local Variable"

print (message2)

#Calling the function myFunction() print("\nOUTSIDE THE FUNCTION")

#Global variables are accessible outside function print (message1)

#Local variables are NOT accessible outside function. print (message2)

If you run the program, you will get the output below.

INSIDE THE FUNCTION

Global Variable Local Variable

OUTSIDE THE FUNCTION

Global Variable

NameError: name 'message2' is not defined

Within the function, both the local and global variables are accessible. Outside the function, the local variable message2 is no longer accessible. We get a NameError when we try to get access to it outside the function.

The second concept to understand about variable scope is that if a local variable shares the same name as a global variable, any code inside the function is accessing the local variable. Any code outside is accessing the global variable. Try to run the code below

message1 = 'Global Variable (shares the same name as a local variable)'

def myFunction():

message1 = 'Local Variable (shares same name as a global variable)'

print("\nINSIDE THE FUNCTION") print (message1)

Calling the function myFunction()

Printing message1 OUTSIDE the function print ("\nOUTSIDE THE FUNCTION") print (message1)

You'll get the output as follows:

INSIDE THE FUNCTION

Local Variable (shares same name as a global variable) OUTSIDE THE FUNCTION

Global Variable (shares same name as a local variable)

When message is printed the function, it prints "Local

Variable (shares same name as a global variable)" as it is printing the local variable. When we print it outside, it is accessing the global variable and hence prints "Global Variable (shares same name as a local variable)".

Importing Modules

Python basically comes with quite a large number of built-in functions. These built-in functions are saved in files known as modules. To utilize the built-in codes in Python modules, we have to import them into our programs first. We do that by using the import keyword. There are three ways to do it.

The first way is to import the entire module by writing import moduleName.

For example, to import the random module, we write import random. To use the randrange() function in the random module, we write random.randrange(1, 10).

If you find it too tedious or stressful to write random each time you use the function, you can import the module by writing import random as r (where r is any name of your choice). Now to use the randrange() function, you simply write r.randrange(1, 10).

The third way to import modules is to import specific functions from the module by writing from moduleName import name1[, name2[, ... nameN]].

For instance, to import the randrange() function from the random module, we write from random import randrange. If we want to import and use more than 1 functions, we separate them with a comma. To import the randrange() and randint() functions, we write from random import randrange, randint. To utilize the function now, we do not have to use the dot notation any longer. Just write randrange(1, 10).

Creating our Own Module

Apart from importing built-in modules, we can also create our personal modules. This is terribly helpful if you have got some functions that you simply need to apply in alternative programming comes in future.

Creating a module is simple. Just save the file with a .py extension and place it in the same folder as the Python file that you are going to import it from.

Suppose you want to use the checkIfPrime() function defined earlier in another Python script. Here's how you do it. To begin with, save the code above as prime.py on your desktop. prime.py should contain the following code.

def checkIfPrime (numberToCheck): for x in range(2, numberToCheck):

if (numberToCheck%x == 0): return False

return True

Next, you should prepare another Python file and name it useCheckIfPrime.py. Save it on your desktop as well. useCheckIfPrime.py should have the following code.

import prime

answer = prime.checkIfPrime(13) print (answer)

Now run useCheckIfPrime.py. You should get the output True. Simple as that.

However, assuming you want to store prime.py and use CheckIfPrime.py in a number different folders. You are going to have to add some codes to use CheckIfPrime.py to tell the Python interpreter where to find the module.

Say you created a folder named 'MyPythonModules' in your C drive to store prime.py. You need to add the following code to the top of your useCheckIfPrime.py file (before the line import prime).

import sys

```python
if 'C:\\MyPythonModules' not in sys.path:
    sys.path.append('C:\\MyPythonModules')
```

sys.path refers to your Python's system path. That is the list of directories that Python scans through to search for modules and files. The above code also appends the folder 'C:\MyPythonModules' to your system path.

Now, you can place prime.py in C:\MyPythonModules and checkIfPrime.py in any other folder of your choice.

Chapter 9: Using Files

Very good! Now we reached the last chapter, before the project. We'll now look at how we can work with external files.

We've seen how to we can get input from the user using input(). But, sometimes, if we need to work with a lot of data, it's more common to use files instead of manual inputs.

This chapter will teach you how!

Reading Files

In this first example, we are going to read from a plain text file. Let's start: create a file with the following text.

Learn Python and Learn It Well

Save this file as myfile.txt in your desktop. Then,open IDLE and write the code below. Save this file as fileOperation.py, again on your desktop.

f = open ('myfile.txt', 'r')

firstline = f.readline()

secondline = f.readline()

print (firstline)

print (secondline) f.close()

The first line has a specific function: open the file.

Before reading from any file, we must open it. The open() function does exactly that.

The 1st parameter is simply the file path.

In case you didn't keep fileOperation.py and myfile.txt in the same directory, you'll need to add, before 'myfile.txt', the full path where you stored the text file. For example, if you saved it in a folder named 'PythonFiles' in your C drive, you need to code 'C:\\PythonFiles\\myfile.txt'.

The other parameter is the file open mode. Commonly used modes are

'r' mode:

For reading only.

'w' mode:

For writing only.

If the desired file doesn't exist, it'll be now created.

If the specified file already exists, existing data on the file will be erased and you'll start with a plain one.

'a' mode:

To append.

If the desired file doesn't exist, it'll be now created.

If the specified file already exists, existing data on the file will be kept and you'll start writing at the bottom of the file.

'r+' mode:

For reading and writing.

After you open the file, the following code

firstline = f.readline()

Is useful to read the first line in the file and assign it to the variable.

Everytime time the readline() function is called, it reads a new line from the file.

In our program, readline() was called two times. So the first two lines will be read.

You'll find that a line break is inserted after every line you write in the file.

This is caused by the readline() function: it automatically adds the '\n' characters to the end of each line. In case you don't want that double line between each line of text, you can execute

print (firstline, end = '').

This will remove the new line characters for the following output.

After reading and printing the two lines, the last line, f.close(), simply closes the file.

You should always close the file once you're done accessing it, so the system can free up some system resources.

Read files with a loop

The readline() function we described above to read a text file, is not enough to read a file with a undefinied row number.

The solution is a loop: here's how you can do that.

f = open ("myfile.txt","r')

for line in f:

print (line, end = '')

f.close()

As you can guess, the loop cycles through the text file, line by line.

Writing to a File

Now that we've discovered how to open and read a file, let's move on and start writing into it.

To do so, we'll use the append mode, identified with 'a'.

It's also possible to use the 'w' mode, that will erase and replace all the content of the file.

f = open ('myfile.txt', 'a')

f.write('\nAny new row will be appended.')

f.write('\nHere is it!')

f.close()

Now we use the write() function to append the two sentences to the file, each starting on a new line entirely because we used the escape characters '\n'.

Challenge Yourself

We've come to the end of this chapter and hopefully you have successfully coded your first program. If you have problems solving any exercise, you can study the answers in Appendix E. You'll learn a lot by taking your time to study other people's codes.

In this section, I have three additional exercises for you to challenge yourself.

Challenge Exercise 1

In the program that we've coded so far, I've avoided using the division operator. Can you modify the program so that it will create questions with the division sign too? How would you check the user's answer against the correct answer?

Hint: Check out the round() function.

Challenge Exercise 2

Sometimes, the question generated may result in an answer that is very large or very small. For example, the question 6*[8^9/1]^3 will give the answer 14507109853755500096474112.

It is very uncomfortable for users to calculate and put in such a large number. Hence, we want to avoid answers that are too big or small. Can you edit the program to prevent questions that brings out answers greater than 50 000 or smaller than -50000?

Challenge Exercise 3

The last challenge exercise is the most difficult.

So far, brackets are missing in the questions generated. Can you modify the program so that the questions use brackets too? An example of a question will be 2 + (3*7 -1) + 5.

Have fun with these exercises. The suggested solution is provided in Appendix E.

Appendix A: Working With Strings

Note: The notation (start,(end))means start and end are choosen parameters. If only one number is provided as the parameter, it is taken to be start.

marks the start of a comment

'" signifies the start and end of a multiline comment. The actual code is in monotype font.

=> marks the start of the output

count (sub, [start, [end]])

Return the number of times the substring sub appears in the string. This function is case-sensitive.

[Example]

In the examples below. 's' occurs at index 3 ,6 and10 # count the entire string

'This is a string'.count('s')

=> 3

count from index 4 to end of string 'This is a string'.count('s', 4) => 2 # count from index 4 to 10-1

'This is a string'. count('s', 4, 10) => 1

count 'T'. There's only one 'T' as the function is case sensitive.

'This is a string'. count('T')

=> 1

endswith (suffix, [start, [end]])

Return the True if the string comes to an end with the specified suffix, otherwise return False.

suffix can also be a tuple of suffixes to search for. This function is case-sensitive.

[Example]

"man"occurs at index 4 to 6# check the entire string

'Postman'.ends with('man')

=> True

check From the index 3 to end of string 'Postman'.ends with('man', 3)

=> True

check from index 2 to 6-1

'Postman'.endswith('man', 2, 6) => False

check from index 2 to 7-1

'Postman'.endswith('man', 2, 7) => True

Using a tuple of suffixes 'Postman'. ends with (('man', 'ma'), 2, 6) => True

find/index (sub, [start, [end]])

Return the index in the string where the first occurrence of the substring sub is found.

find() returns -1 if sub is not found.

index() returns ValueError is sub is not found. This function is case-sensitive.

[Example]

check the entire string

'This is a string'.find('s')

=> 3

check from index 4 to end of string 'This is a string'.find('s', 4) => 6 # check from index 7 to 11-1

'This is a string'.find('s', 7,11) => 10

Sub is not found

'This is a string'.find('p')

=> -1

'This is a string'.index('p')

=> ValueError

isalnum()

Return the true if all characters in the string are alphanumerics and there is at least one character, false the otherwise.

Alphanumeric does not include whitespaces.

[Example]

'abcd1234'.isalnum()

=> True

'a b c d 1 2 3 4'.isalnum()

=> False

'abcd'.isalnum()

=> True

'1234'.isalnum()

=> True

isalpha()

Return the true if all the characters in the string are in alphabet format and there is at least one character, false the otherwise.

[Example]

'abcd'.isalpha()

=> True

'abcd1234'.isalpha()

=> False

'1234'.isalpha()

=> False

'a b c'.isalpha()

=> False

isdigit()

Return the true if all the characters in the string are all digits and there is at least one character, false the otherwise.

[Example]

'1234'.isdigit()

=> True

'abcd1234'.isdigit()

=> False

'abcd'.isdigit()

=> False

'1 2 3 4'.isdigit()

=> False

islower()

Return the true if all cased characters in the string are lowercase and there is at least one cased character, false otherwise.

[Example]

'abcd'.islower()

=> True

'Abcd'.islower()

=> False

'ABCD'.islower()

=> False

isspace()

Return the true if all are only whitespace characters in the string and there is at least one character, false otherwise.

[Example]

' '.isspace()

=> True

'a b'.isspace()

=> False

istitle()

Return the true if the string is a titlecased string and there is at least one character

[Example]

'This Is A String'.istitle()

=> True

'This is a string'.istitle()

=> False

isupper()

Return true if all cased characters in the string are all uppercase and there is at least one cased character, false otherwise.

[Example]

'ABCD'.isupper()

=> True

'Abcd'.isupper()

=> False

'abcd'.isupper()

=> False

join()

Return a single string in which the parameter given is joined by a separator.
[Example]

sep = '-'

myTuple = ('a', 'b', 'c')

myList = ['d', 'e', 'f'] myString = "Hello World"

sep.join(myTuple)

=> 'a-b-c'

sep.join(myTuple)

=> 'd-e-f'

sep.join(myString)

=> 'H-e-l-l-o- -W-o-r-l-d"

lower()

Return a single copy of the string converted to the lowercase. [Example]

'Hello Python'.lower()

=> 'hello python'

replace(old, new[, count])

Return a single copy of the string with all occurrences of substring old replaced by new.

count is optional. If given, only the first count occurrences are replaced. This function is case-sensitive.

[Example]

Replace all occurences

'This is a string'.replace('s', 'p') => 'Thip ip a ptring'

Replace first 2 occurences

'This is a string'.replace('s', 'p', 2) => 'Thip ip a string'

split([sep [,maxsplit]])

Return a single list of the words in the string, using the sep as the delimiter string.

sep and maxsplit are optional.

If sep is not given, whitespace is used as the delimiter. if maxsplit is provided, at most maxsplit are done.

This function is case-sensitive. [Example]

'''

Split using comma (,) as the delimiter signal that there's a space provided before the words 'is', 'a' and 'string' in the outcome.

'''

"This, is, a, string". split(',') => ['This', ' is', ' a', ' string']

Split using whitespace as delimiter 'This is a string'.split()

=> ['This', 'is', 'a', 'string']

Only do 2 splits

'This, is, a,. "string". split(',' 2) => ['This', ' is', ' a, string']

splitlines ([keepends])

Return a single list of the lines in the string, breaking at the line boundaries.

Linebreaks are not mentioned in the resulting list unless keep ends is provided and true.

[Example]

Split lines separated by \n

'This is the first line.\nThis is the second line'.splitlines() => ['This is the first line.', 'This is the second line.']

Split multi line string (e.g. string that uses the "mark)" 'This is the first line.

This is the second line."'.splitlines() => ['This is the first line.', 'This is the second line.']

Split and keep line breaks

'This is the first line.\nThis is the second line.'.splitlines(True) => ['This is the first line.\n', 'This is the second line.']

'''This is the first line.

This is the second line.'''.splitlines(True) => ['This is the first line.\n', 'This is the second line.']

startswith (prefix[, start[, end]])

Return the True if string starts with the prefix, or otherwise return False.

prefix could also be a tuple of prefixes to look for. This function is case-sensitive.

[Example]

'Post' occurs at index 0 to 3 # check the entire string

'Postman'.startswith('Post')

=> True

check from index 3 to end of string 'Postman'.startswith('Post', 3) =>

False

check from index 2 to 6-1

'Postman'.startswith('Post', 2, 6) => False

check from index 2 to 6-1

'Postman'.startswith('stm', 2, 6) => True

Using a tuple of prefixes (check from index 3 to end of string) 'Postman'.startswith(('Post', 'tma'), 3) => True

strip ([chars])

Return a single copy of the string with the leading and trailing characters char removed.

If char is not provided, whitespaces will be removed. This function is case-sensitive.

[Example]

Strip whitespaces

' This, is, a, string '.strip() => 'This is a string'

Strip 's'. Nothing is removed since 's' is not at the start or end of the string
'This is a string'.strip('s')

=> 'This is a string'

Strip 'g'.

'This is a string'.strip('g')

=> 'This is a strin'

upper()

Return a single copy of the string converted to uppercase. [Example]

'Hello Python'.upper()

=> 'HELLO PYTHON'

Appendix B: Working With Lists

=> marks the start of the output

append( )

Add item to the end of a list

[Example]

myList = ['a', 'b', 'c', 'd'] myList.append('e') print (myList)

=> ['a', 'b', 'c', 'd', 'e']

del

Remove items from a list

[Example]

myList = ['a', 'b', 'c', 'd', 'e', 'f', 'g', 'h', 'i', 'j', 'k', 'l']

#delete the third item (index = 2) del myList[2]

print (myList)

=> ['a','b','d','e','f','g','h','i','j','k','l']

#delete items from index 1 to 5-1

del myList[1:5] print (myList)

=> ['a', 'g', 'h', 'i', 'j', 'k', 'l']

#delete items from index 0 to 3-1

del myList [:3] print (myList)

=> ['i', 'j', 'k', 'l']

#delete items from index 2 to end del myList [2:]

print (myList)

=> ['i', 'j']

extend( )

Combine two lists

[Example]

myList = ['a', 'b', 'c', 'd', 'e'] myList2 = [1, 2, 3, 4]

myList.extend(myList2) print (myList)

=> ['a', 'b', 'c', 'd', 'e', 1, 2, 3, 4]

In

Check if an item is in a list

[Example]

myList = ['a', 'b', 'c', 'd'] 'c' in myList

=> True

'e' in myList

=> False

insert( )

Add item to a list at a particular position

[Example]

myList = ['a', 'b', 'c', 'd', 'e'] myList.insert(1, 'Hi') print (myList)

=> ['a', 'Hi', 'b', 'c', 'd', 'e']

len( )

Find the number of items in a list [Example]

myList = ['a', 'b', 'c', 'd'] print (len(myList)) => 4

pop( )

Get the value of an item and remove it from the list Requires index of item as the parameter

[Example]

myList = ['a', 'b', 'c', 'd', 'e']

#remove the third item member = myList.pop(2) print (member)

=> c

print (myList)

=> ['a', 'b', 'd', 'e']

#remove the last item member = myList.pop( ) print (member)

=> e

print (myList)

=> ['a', 'b', 'd']

remove( )

Remove an item from a list. Requires the value of the item as the parameter.

[Example]

myList = ['a', 'b', 'c', 'd', 'e']

#remove the item 'c'

myList.remove('c') print (myList)

=> ['a', 'b', 'd', 'e']

reverse()

Reverse the items in a list

[Example]

myList = [1, 2, 3, 4] myList.reverse() print (myList)

=> [4, 3, 2, 1]

sort()

Sort a list alphabetically or numerically

[Example]

myList = [3, 0, -1, 4, 6]

myList.sort() print(myList)

=> [-1, 0, 3, 4, 6]

sorted()

Return a new sorted list without sorting the original list.

Requires a list as the parameter [Example]

myList = [3, 0, -1, 4, 6]

myList2 = sorted(myList)

#Original list is not sorted print (myList)

=> [3, 0, -1, 4, 6]

#New list is sorted print (myList2)

=> [-1, 0, 3, 4, 6]

Addition Operator: +

Concatenate List [Example]

myList = ['a', 'b', 'c', 'd']

print (myList + ['e', 'f']) => ['a', 'b', 'c', 'd', 'e', 'f']

print (myList)

=> ['a', 'b', 'c', 'd']

Multiplication Operator: *

Duplicate a list and concatenate it to the end of the list [Example]

myList = ['a', 'b', 'c', 'd'] print (myList*3)

=> ['a', 'b', 'c', 'd', 'a', 'b', 'c', 'd', 'a', 'b', 'c', 'd']

print (myList)

=> ['a', 'b', 'c', 'd']

Note:

The + and * symbols do not modify the list. The list stays as ['a', 'b', 'c','d'] in both cases.

Appendix C: Working With Tuples

=> marks the start of the output

del

Delete the entire tuple

[Example]

myTuple = ('a', 'b', 'c', 'd') del myTuple

print (myTuple) => NameError: name 'myTuple' is not defined

in

Check if an item is in a tuple [Example]

myTuple = ('a', 'b', 'c', 'd') 'c' in myTuple => True 'e' in myTuple => False

len( )

Find the number of items in a tuple [Example]

myTuple = ('a', 'b', 'c', 'd') print (len(myTuple)) => 4

Addition Operator: +

Concatenate Tuples

[Example]

myTuple = ('a', 'b', 'c', 'd') print (myTuple + ('e',

'f')) => ('a', 'b', 'c', 'd', 'e', 'f')

print (myTuple) => ('a', 'b', 'c', 'd')

Multiplication Operator: *

Duplicate a tuple and concatenate it to the end of the tuple [Example]

myTuple = ('a', 'b', 'c', 'd') print(myTuple*3) => ('a', 'b', 'c', 'd', 'a', 'b', 'c', 'd', 'a', 'b', 'c', 'd')

print (myTuple) => ('a', 'b', 'c', 'd')

Note: The + and * symbols do not modify the tuple. The tuple stays as ['a', 'b', 'c', 'd'] in both cases.

Appendix D: Working With Dictionaries

=> marks the start of the output

clear( )

Removes all elements of the dictionary, returning an empty dictionary [Example]

dic1 = {1: 'one', 2: 'two'} print (dic1)

=> {1: 'one', 2: 'two'}

dic1.clear() print (dic1)

=> { }

del

Delete the entire dictionary [Example]

dic1 = {1: 'one', 2: 'two'} del dic1

print (dic1)

=> NameError: name 'dic1' is not defined

get( )

Returns a value for the given key.

If the key is not found, it'll return the keyword None.

Alternatively, you can state the value to return if the key is not found.

[Example]

dic1 = {1: 'one', 2: 'two'} dic1.get(1)

=> 'one'

dic1.get(5)

=> None

dic1.get(5, "Not Found") => 'Not Found'

In

Check if an item is in a dictionary [Example]

dic1 = {1: 'one', 2: 'two'}

based on the key 1 in dic1

=> True

3 in dic1

=> False

based on the value 'one' in dic1.values() => True 'three' in dic1.values() => False **items( )**

Returns a list of dictionary's pairs as tuples

[Example]

dic1 = {1: 'one', 2: 'two'} dic1.items()

=> dict_items([(1, 'one'), (2, 'two')])

keys( )

Returns list of the dictionary's keys [Example]

dic1 = {1: 'one', 2: 'two'} dic1.keys()

=> dict_keys([1, 2])

len( )

Find the number of items in a dictionary [Example]

dic1 = {1: 'one', 2: 'two'} print (len(dic1)) => 2

update( )

Adds one dictionary's key-values pairs to another. Duplicates are removed.

[Example]

dic1 = {1: 'one', 2: 'two'}

dic2 = {1: 'one', 3: 'three'}

dic1.update(dic2) print (dic1)

=> {1: 'one', 2: 'two', 3: 'three'}

print (dic2) #no change => {1: 'one', 3: 'three'}

values( )

Returns list of the dictionary's values [Example]

dic1 = {1: 'one', 2: 'two'} dic1.values()

=> dict_values(['one', 'two'])

Appendix E: Project Answers

<u>Exercise 1</u>

from random import randint from os import remove, rename

Exercise 2

def getUserScore(userName):

try:

input = open('userScores.txt', 'r') for line in input:

content = line.split(',') if content[0] == userName:

input.close() return content[1]

input.close() return "-1"

except IOError:

print ("\nFile userScores.txt not found. a new file will be made.'). input =

open('userScores.txt', 'w')

input.close() return "-1"

Exercise 3

def updateUserPoints(newUser, userName, score): if newUser:

input = open('userScores.txt', 'a') input.write('\n' + userName + ',' + score)

input.close()

else:

input = open('userScores.txt', 'r') output = open('userScores.tmp', 'w')

for line in input:

```python
content = line.split(',') if content[0] == userName:

content[1] = score

line = content[0] +','+content[1] + '\n'

output.write(line) input.close() output.close()


remove('userScores.txt') rename('userScores.tmp', 'userScores.txt')
```

Exercise 4

```python
def generateQuestion():

operandList = [0, 0, 0, 0, 0] operatorList = ['', '', '', '']

operatorDict = {1:'+',2:' -', 3:'',4:'*'}

for index in range(0, 5): operandList[index] = randint(1, 9)

for index in range(0, 4):

if index > 0 and operatorList[index-1] != '**': operator = operatorDict[randint(1, 4)]

else: operator = operatorDict[randint(1, 3)]

operatorList[index] = operator questionString = str(operandList[0])

for index in range(1, 5): questionString = questionString +

operatorList[index-1] + str(operandList[index]) result = eval(questionString)

questionString = questionString.replace("**", "^") print ('\n' + questionString)

userResult = input('Answer: ')
while True:
try:
```

if int(userResult) == result:

print . ('So Smart') return 1 else: print ("Sorry, wrong

answer. The correct answer is", result)

return 0

Remove Exception as e: print ("You did not enter a number. Please try again.")

userResult = input('Answer: ')

[Explanation for Exercise 9.2]

Starting from the second item (i.e. index = 1) in operatorList, the line if index > 0 and operatorList[index-1] != '**': checks if the previous item in operatorList is the '**' symbol..

If not, the statement operator = operator Dict[randint (1, 4)] will execute. Since the range given to the randint function is 1 to 4, the numbers 1, 2, 3 or 4 will be generated. Hence, the symbols '+', '-', '' or '*' will be assigned to the variable operator.

However, if the previous symbol is '**', the else statement (operator = operatorDict[randint(1, 3)]) will execute. In this case, the range given to the randint function is from 1 to 3. Hence, the '**' symbol, which has a key of 4 in operatorDict will NOT be assigned to the operator variable.

Exercise 5

try:

import myPythonFunctions as m

userName = input('''Please enter your user name or create a new one if this is the first time you are running the program: ''')

userScore = int(m.getUserScore(userName)) if userScore == -1:

newUser = True userScore = 0

else:

newUser = False

userChoice = 0

while userChoice != '-1':

userScore += m.generateQuestion() print ("Current Score = ", userScore) userChoice = input("Press Enter To Continue or -1 to Exit: ")

m.updateUserPoints(newUser, userName, str(userScore))

except Exception as e:

print ("An unexpected error occurred. Program will be exited.")

Conclusion

Python is a powerful programming language and gives a simple use of the code lines, maintenance can be dealt with in an extraordinary manner, and debugging or investigation of code should be possible effectively as well. It has picked up significance over the globe as PC mammoth Google has made it one of its official programming languages.

So, we've come to the end of the book and I am sure this book will give you all that are required to jump on the python programming language and explore further.

Thank you for reading this book and I hope you have enjoyed the book. More importantly, I sincerely hope the book has helped you master the fundamentals of Python programming.

Don't miss out!

Visit the website below and you can sign up to receive emails whenever Kevin Lioy publishes a new book. There's no charge and no obligation.

https://books2read.com/r/B-A-HSOR-PHOYC

Connecting independent readers to independent writers.

Did you love *Python for Beginners: The Dummies' Guide to Learn Python Programming. A Practical Reference with Exercises for Newbies and Advanced Developers*? Then you should read *WordPress for Beginners: The Complete Dummies Guide to Start Your Own Blog From Zero to Advanced Development and Customization. Includes Plugin and SEO Techniques to Kickstart Your Business.*[1] by Kevin Lioy!

[2]

If you want to discover the most famous Blogging Platform in the World, then keep reading.

WordPress is a website platform allowing anyone - literally, anyone - to have a blog up and running in a few minutes.

But you have to know how to set-up, manage and use it!

WordPress is quite easy to use, but it's extremely powerful. It has thousands different functions and it's also easy to expand thanks to the millions of plugins already available today.

In this book you will discover...

---

1. https://books2read.com/u/4Nynw6

2. https://books2read.com/u/4Nynw6

▶ Why WordPress is the best platform for your blog▶ *How to setup WordPress, step by step*▶ How to increase the performance of your website with advanced techniques▶ *The importance of having a backup - always*▶ How to actually use the platform▶ *How to analyze the data to increase your traffic*▶ How to publish your content▶ *The best methods to handle your community*▶ The SEO-friendly way to use categories and tags▶ *The best plugins to create photo galleries, podcasts and any other content*▶ The WordPress community and why it's so important▶ *How to use WordPress as a CMS to create any kind of website*

Also by Kevin Lioy

Programmazione per Principianti
Python: La Guida Per Imparare a Programmare. Include Esercizi di
Programmazione.

Programmazione Web
MySQL: Database SQL per Principanti
PHP: Sviluppo Web Lato Server
NodeJS: Programmare Web-App Con Javascript

Python Programming
Python for Beginners: The Dummies' Guide to Learn Python Programming.
A Practical Reference with Exercises for Newbies and Advanced Developers

WordPress Programming
WordPress for Beginners: The Complete Dummies Guide to Start Your Own
Blog From Zero to Advanced Development and Customization. Includes
Plugin and SEO Techniques to Kickstart Your Business.
Blogging for Beginners: The Dummies Guide to Start a Business Blog from
Scratch, Become a Niche Influencer with SEO and Social Media and Profit
from Affiliate Marketing

About the Author

Kevin Lioy has written more than a dozen books on programming and similar topics.